Contents

Introduction

This small book reflects the work and contribution of many different people in the history of Indian dance and music in Leicester since the 1960s. It shows that from humble beginnings soon after the migration of more South Asian people to Leicester, dance has played an increasingly important role in the life of the community. Today's Leicester is quite different from what it used to be a few decades earlier. Side by side with its older historical foundations, it is increasingly obvious that the city's lively Asian cultural scene is making important contributions to tourism and economic development. We are rightly proud in Leicester of having found a way to combine East and West.

I came to Leicester in September 1980, after a long performance tour in Germany and soon found that the facilities for teaching and performing Indian dance in Leicester were totally underdeveloped. Some enterprising people would create ad hoc dances on certain occasions for community events or festivals. Some teaching was offered at community centres, but there was no continuity, no overall structure for any long-term development. There had been interesting dance events like the Raas and Garba competitions of the 1970s, but they had collapsed for various reasons. In the early 1980s, the video culture was booming and people were spending their leisure time in front of 'the box' rather than learning anything about dance.

While I had found London too much like Bombay, Leicester reminded me of my native city, Baroda, a lively cultural and educational centre. There I had trained for many years in Kathak dance, graduating from diploma and BMus studies to a Masters degree in Kathak at the famous Music College of Baroda University. Having run my own dance school in India earlier, I ventured to open the Institute of Classical Indian Dance in Leicester on 1 January 1981, in a space which must have seen many changes - from being a factory to a Polish shop and now a training centre and rehearsal space for Indian dance.

The central aim has been to promote cultural awareness and knowledge of Kathak dance in this new environment. Very quickly, my work as a performer and teacher began to flourish not only locally but also regionally and nationally. Today, Leicester is a major, if not the leading, national centre for Asian dance and music in Britain. This flourishing development has been made possible by the sustained effort of many different people and organisations, large and small, right down to the seven-year olds who are now experiencing their first few formal lessons in Kathak dance.

In 1985, Leicester established the Asian Dance Animateur project, co-funded by the City, County and, for an initial period, East Midlands Arts and the Arts Council of Great Britain. This pioneering project established a formal framework for the continuing growth of South Asian dance activities in the Midlands. We trained a large number of dance students and for most people this was an interesting hobby and, increasingly, an exciting chance to perform. Some of the early students are now working as dance tutors within the community, not only in Leicester but also in Nottingham,

London and elsewhere. Since 1991, I have been Leicester City Council's Asian Dance Development Officer. It is good to see that despite all kinds of difficulties Asian dance work has continued to flourish. Today, the city has nine centres in which classical, folk and creative Indian dance forms are regularly taught.

The prominent position of Leicester in the field of South Asian dance may not be obvious to local people, but it is not surprising and not by chance. Solid training and structured practical and theoretical education in Indian dance for the past fifteen years is gradually beginning to bear visible fruits. In 1994 and 1995, two young Kathak dancers from Leicester won the prestigious National Scholarships of ADiTi, the Association of South Asian Dancers, to train in India full-time for one year. Currently, three of our dance tutors are taking part in a pioneering South Asian Dance Artists in Schools course at a London university. This also reflects the fact that South Asian dance input has increasingly become an integral part of Leicester's mainstream provision in dance education. From being just a colourful adjunct, we have moved to the centre of exciting developments of which people in other cities are increasingly aware.

Working as a professional Kathak dancer and teacher in Leicester since 1981, I have seen many changes, from the early beginnings to today's sell-out performances in the city's theatres. It occurred to me that the story of this development should be recorded and written up for a wider public and this suggestion was positively received by the city's Living History Unit, whose work I greatly admire. It is important, especially for younger people, that we preserve records of how the present achievements have been built up from small beginnings. In many ways, this shows the truth of the old saying that 'where there's a will there's a way'. Hopefully the present collection of material will encourage and inspire others to paint a fuller picture yet than we could possibly achieve at this stage.

Due credit and many thanks must be given to the Living History Unit at Leicester City Council, especially Angela Cutting, one of the Living History Officers, as well as Smita Vadnerkar and Colin Hyde, who conducted the oral interviews on which this book is based. Finally, all those who contributed to this project by generously giving their time, pictures and other material, and by sharing their memories with us, deserve special thanks.

Nilima Devi

Nilima Devi

The 1960s

'Everyone would dash off to the cinemas'

Immigrants from the Indian sub-continent started to arrive in Leicester from the late 1940s. Sikhs from the Punjab in North West India formed the major part of the Asian community in Leicester during the 1950s. Then followed people from Gujarat, Pakistan and what is now known as Bangladesh, and the 1960s and '70s saw the arrival of Asians from East Africa. For the early small groups of settlers the opportunities to take part in traditional social and arts events were very few, and celebration of religious festivals was generally small and low-key. For many people going to the cinema was the only form of art available.

When I came here in 1964 there were people here... there were some organisations who were involved in setting up the local groups to organise cultural and religious events in the city. I can remember... the first cultural programme I have seen in Leicester was the Indian Independence Day. That was organised by India Link in 1964, and also in 1965. I was very impressed by that you see. They first started... by inviting these guests from the Indian Embassy in London and also they invited the local MPs. The cultural programme consisted of classical music and also Indian folk dances and Raas, but at that time there was a very limited population... Corporation Hall – it is now a warehouse – on the Belgrave roundabout by the fly-over. That was very well organised.

In 1965 or '66 we held our first Navratri in Leicester; that was at Charnwood school, and also St. Mark's Church.

The Gujarat Hindu Association was formed, which was an umbrella organisation for all the organisations. Before that was the Indo-African Society and the Indian National Club, they were mostly all showing the films... and that was the only entertainment for the Asian community in Leicester at that time. Every Sunday and Saturday... if you want to find your Asian friend, you'd find them near the cinema.

At the Gujarati school we did organise a small cultural programme for children. We started training children - Garba and small dances, you see. That started coming from the Gujarati school which is called the Indian Educational Society. It's been in existence for 30 years now. The Gujarat Hindu Association was formed in, somewhere near 1970, 1972.

When I came here (1964) they used to celebrate India Republic Day, Independence Day, that kind of function used to take place and I used to sing there. They asked me to organise various activities, which I did.

At that time there wasn't particularly any religious group you could go to because there weren't enough people. There used to be some Sikhs, they used to have their temple - it wasn't a building, they used to meet in a school on a Sunday morning.

The Asian cultural life was literally non-existent in 1968, even celebrations, even weddings, it was very difficult to hold, I know there was nothing like the present celebrations in weddings... they would just have a little diva and conduct the ceremony round that... everybody was new, they were all trying to get established; the contacts - they didn't have much contact with other people, also the non-availability of a lot of the stuff required, and the priests and things. Those were also the problems at that time. Also, I mean getting halls was very difficult and of course expense must have been another factor because people were trying to get themselves established, settled down. So they tried to keep it simple, which in a way was good.

I know how starved the Asians would feel because everyone would dash off to cinemas, I mean there used to be two shows per ticket, and the main idea of going to cinemas was partly to be exposed to the culture and partly also to be able to meet other fellow Asians, because they were starved in both ways - culturally and company-wise.

Perhaps during Navratri small groups might have got together and celebrated those, perhaps even in private homes, but there was nothing like the present day Navratri celebrations we see. I'm talking from the schools' point of view - there was very little happening in schools, almost nothing you could say.

There used to be generally two films shown at the same time, one after the other, and Indian films are generally of three hours duration, and you can just imagine going at about twelve o'clock and coming out of the hall at about six o'clock. That used to be Sunday - the most enjoyment, that's all we had. We couldn't go anywhere else 'cos there was nothing going on; these festivals would take place perhaps annually, one or two, and if by chance you missed one you haven't got any other coming there. The only art we saw was on the cinema screen.

Especially if you are a person who is a vegetarian, a person who doesn't particularly want to go to pubs for drinking, you haven't got any social life. The social life here was that people used to say, 'Let's go to the pub', and people like me who didn't drink at all, there was no life at all.

I think the main festivals were celebrated fairly well at the time, I mean Diwali, Navratri... the main festivals of the Hindus in particular. As regards to the festivities, they went on in the temples at the time, there were some occasions when they were put up on stages like the neighbourhood centres and some of the temple halls. There were very few schools who recognised the festivities at that stage but I do know there were one or two schools who had a high percentage of Asians who had started having dances and festivities regarding Diwali... and all the others as well.

I think it was mostly very individual. The families who had the musical instruments, they would encourage the families nearby or the closest relatives to try and take part in bhajans and kirtans, music of that sort. Then, obviously, there was the folk dance and the folk lore, and the film songs was the other element that was occasionally put on stage. There were very few communities who had organised in detail. It was very early days so you wouldn't expect the standards to be anywhere near what we know of it now.

The 1970s

'We used to hire De Montfort Hall, it used to get packed'

From the late 1960s into the '70s people began arriving in Leicester from Kenya, Uganda and Tanzania. Folk dancing, such as Raas and Garba, became very popular and competitions were often organised by new groups such as the Gujarat Hindu Association. Many Leicester performers went on to win top prizes in national competitions.

I came to Leicester... in 1972, from Germany, as a student in fact, but I had a job here to teach at City of Leicester and Alderman Newton's schools. Of course in September 1972 it was exactly when Idi Amin was throwing out the Ugandan Asians and so very interesting things happened at exactly that time. From day one I met a lot of Asian people because I ended up at the YMCA sharing a room with some Asians. I was instantly involved in a lot of Gujarati activities.

At that time, Asian cultural life, one could talk about two things. One was that a lot of film activities were going on - you had all these big cinemas which are now all dead... at that stage still you had a very vibrant cinema culture. On weekends people would just go to the Coliseum on Melton Road, or Anand Cinema in Green Lane Road or what have you. I found this fascinating, they were really family events and family affairs.

Leicester Mercury

A group of boys from Soar Valley School who gave a display of Bhangra dancing at Wembley Conference Centre, London in 1982.

The Shree Sarvoday Samaj dance troupe won some of the top prizes in the
14th annual Raas and Garba competition at De Montfort Hall in 1984.

When it came to dance events I remember going with my Gujarati friends to dance events at De Montfort Hall which were huge, which were big, and they were, you know, explicitly multicultural, they were sort of taster sessions for everybody to get to know a little bit about different forms of dance and different forms of cultures in the same way. So there was a sort of performing group there that did this dance but then... there was this interplay of a little performance and then public participation. This involved, as far as I remember, stick dancing... Bhangra... Scottish dance, Irish dance, Polish dance, I remember. It must have been '72, '73, and possibly again '75. '76.

I do remember that there were Raas and Garba competitions - Gujarati folk dance competitions.

It is word of mouth but it is also institutionalised community links, you know, the Patels are doing this and the Sonis are doing that. Certainly when it comes to those Raas and Garba competitions that was very much community against community, it was warfare, you know, in a different media. Very clearly, you know. It's still like that of course, yes it's no different now.

I think at that early stage there was very little formal training, it was folk dance, it was sort of passed on from mother to daughter, from friend to friend, word of mouth in a sense again, not formal structured training as it is now. Now there is much more emphasis on classical dance, which wasn't there at that time. Before it was all folk, it was mixed things... it was film dance a lot because people watched all these films and you had all these things going on there that people sort of recreated on stage.

When the people started coming from Kenya and East Africa we started inviting people for a Gujarati play, or a Hindi play... and the play was organised at the Queens Hall, a long time ago, at the University, and that was the first play. After the play we thought let's try a Raas and Garba competition, and the first competition was held in, I think it was 1972... it was successful, first year was successful... for six or seven years it went very well. We used to hire De Montfort Hall, it used to get packed.

I think the standard in the beginning was a little bit higher, then it dropped down. After seven years the competition ran down because there was a lot of conflict... because who gets the prize and all that, there was a lot of problems there. So we stopped the competition you see.

The difficulties were, who gets the prize? Why? The adjudicators have not done the marks properly or something like that... 'Cos we have performed best'... some of the people think you belong to that organisation so the prizes must have been fixed.

We told them... adjudicators are all independent! We started with the UK... first few years people came from London, Preston, Birmingham, Coventry, everywhere. Even now the competition is very popular in Leicester... people want to come from outside but we can't cater for them.

Then when I became the secretary of the Gujarat Hindu Association in 1989 I started reviving again the competition. From then we had no problems.

Well, when I came to Leicester there was not too much happening at the time. I was eventually going to settle in London... but one of my students, she was taking part in a Raas and Garba festival at De Montfort Hall in 1970, and she heard that I was in the UK and she somehow managed to get in touch with me, and then she invited me to her house... and she wanted me to help her as a musician. There was a cultural life - not too much - but it was actually beginning. I don't remember who was teaching Raas Garba at that time but a few girls, friends who were keen on dancing, got together and they choreographed themselves... and I was invited to compose music for the dance. So like that the interest grew. Then from that group, a few other groups emerged, you know, like that it grew and grew... that's why Raas Garba flourished in Leicester, and eventually... Kathak emerged, and slowly Bharatnatyam emerged like that. So people have now got a choice.

Then I came to know a few friends who were interested in doing some musical sittings at parties... and then we all gathered one day and we formed a musical group and we used to practise every day at St Peter's church. It was very limited, there weren't many people here at that time, and there were a few keen musicians and singers.

It was a very difficult life you see at that time. There were not proper musicians available, there were a few you know, a few friends who knew a few songs, like bhajans and film songs, and when we met together... the life was so lonely here we used to gather every night and we used to play music and sing and kill our time like that. It was just the very beginning.

I started teaching you see, a few friends, and then gradually I was known by people in Leicester... I got a part-time job at Charles Keene College as a music teacher. I made my name there. We used to do concerts... beginners who never knew what music was... I taught them and then at the end of the term we used to do concerts.

There was the difficulty of having venues, places to get together. People used to celebrate like, I remember in the '60s, a few women would get together at someone's house and they used to have a dance, or Garba, just for Navratri. Similarly, the men used to gather in one small house and they start doing the bhajans or kirtans. These are the ways they started in their own way. As the community becomes bigger and bigger... they found some places like halls... and they started celebrating.

In the beginning, you know, we had to go search for a person who knew a little bit about the tabla, harmonium, music or singing. We had to go to him and request, and please come and help us, or do this performance, and we had to provide the transport also to these persons because it was very difficult in those days, there wasn't enough transport in the '70s. So, creative people, we had to bring them and they were very shy, they were not very willing to come to the stage or do the things, but slowly they just came. Now, a few of them, I know them, they became professional artists... the same people who were very shy to go on the stage in the 1970s, now in the '80s and '90s, they are now professional - they are not available... 'Sorry, we've got no time at the moment.

I came to Leicester from Uganda in 1972... because there were lots of problems... by General Idi Amin. When I came in October the Navratri festival had just started and I happened to go to Granby Halls and to my amazement it was packed out with lots of Asian people from all over the country in fact,

Navratri celebrations at Granby Halls

because it was supposed to be one of the biggest held Navratri events since Leicester is the most ethnic minority place. The music was live and everybody was playing traditional Raas and Garba. The new thing I saw at that time was that the Raas and Garba was played by mixed gender, where back home in Uganda, and what I've heard in India, that people did not play together... men used to play separate from the female. The different thing here was that everyone played together.

People were very traditional, nothing was new. It was Navratri period, Diwali period, and the Raas Garba competition, it wasn't an ongoing thing.

There wasn't anything available professionally, people used to get together and prepare their own Raas Garba items to perform for mandirs, or any openings, but they were very basic and they had to use recorded music - very traditional recorded music - there wasn't much available, even in the cassette form. There were people like Viran Bhatt, who used to come from London from 1973 to teach us Rajasthani dances. That was the first time I had heard about Rajasthan - the name, the song, the style - we used to perform. There used to be a lot of activity going on at the Alankar Sari House, they used to invite people to come to their shop... and we used to have private functions at their house where we used to do music with people from outside England, and we used to have small concerts and... short things, family things, for about 50 - 100 people. Not classical, there were ghazal singers, bhajan singers, and folk singers but not at the level you get these days.

We used to have fancy dress during Navratri festival... best costume, best dress. We used to prepare our own movements, our own styles, a group of 12-15 girls aged between 15-20, and we used to literally show off when we went to Granby Halls and De Montfort Hall - those were the two main venues where these events took place. Huge audiences used to come. Mainly it was folk dance based.

I have older sisters... they were in this group called Milan Arts and each time they used to come back with first prize in costume and at the time we had to prepare own costumes. We had to prepare them from stuff that we had in our houses, and prepare cones and everything, you know. Everything was hand made and the music was slightly changed because live musicians were going to sing. It was very social to go out and meet these people who were also interested, because when you come to a strange country you feel everybody's going to be strange, but having found people who were culturally rooted it was very nice.

Yes, things did happen, bhajans did happen, dances did happen, but people used to do them in their homes because they didn't know who to get into contact with so it used to happen in small pockets.

I wasn't aware of any cultural side because I was... very busy working. But at that time there wasn't any publicity like radios... so I wasn't aware at that time. I heard there was a competition but there was no publicity material.

After 1975, '76, there were more visits from the Indian sub-continent from people who were expert on the front of dance in particular, and even on the music front we had groups of people, parties, we had individual persons from colleges of dance from Delhi or Bombay visiting Leicester. They used to come to visit the UK overall... and they used to show some of the dance on the television and it is from there the interest grew, and I think it is that... that made Leicester... realise that they had to bring their dances up to the level of the experts who were bringing in the talent.

Taking dance and music into the schools

'It was a great boost to their morale'

As more schools began to introduce the celebration of traditional Indian festivals, so the realisation grew that dance and music played a vital role in the expression of those celebrations.

A local youth Bhangra group

Leicester City Council

I initially started in a completely all white school, so at that time the scope seemed very little there. Soon I got myself transferred to the Highfields area where there was a fair mixture at that time, it wasn't completely Asian, there were quite a few English as well as West Indian. So I started in very simple ways there and it really took off. That sort of showed me what need there was and demand there was for this sort of thing. Then towards the mid-'70s they started organising competitions and that for Asian youths, and they would select them out of every region and then have a big show at the Albert Hall. I entered my school children - who were junior school children at the time - twice for this competition and they won it both times and they represented the Midlands at the Albert Hall. That was a fantastic experience for these children, and for myself of course, and from there it just sort of rolled on. There were invites from all over the country, literally. The best for the children was to be invited to universities... they would perform there, and the standard was very high, and then of course the older university students would make all the fuss, you know, and they would put them up for the night and look after them, and the kids were really over the moon for this sort of thing.

The dances; I started with the boys groups, teaching them Bhangra, which was very popular, then we started onto girls groups as well. We did the usual, the stick dance - the Raas Garba - that was very popular and then gradually we brought in some other film cum religious type of songs, like Gangamaiya, doing the diva dance... there were some film songs as well.

In the schools you could see if you mentioned anything Indian or Asian in the early '70s the children would literally get embarrassed and that was partly because they were being picked upon as well, so we wanted to make them develop some sort of pride in them for the culture, for the language and everything. So besides dance I also tried to make sure that

Piali Ray working with a group of schoolchildren

Piali Ray

we used language in the schools... not only that I would try to tell them stories during assembly time. This way, the more they heard the more this feeling of embarrassment was got rid of and they started coming out more and more with their own languages... I mean, we made sure we used a lot of Indian music in schools during assembly times. This was a great boost to their morale at that time.

I was very keen to try and buy some instruments for the school and I invited a person called Mr Bharat to try and bring just two or three instruments like the sitar and the naal and the harmonium, and a few manjiras and things like that, to try and introduce some form of Asian music on the periphery of the main music curriculum itself. And when Dr Choudhri from Delhi came along, I think by that time we had three or four peripatetic music teachers established by the Leicester education authority. By '75, '76 the music was very well established. It was a complement to the work which I was already doing, mind you, mine was more of a folky dance music whereas the one that was being brought in was real standardised tabla lessons... children had to study accordingly. I still remember asking some of the children, who very early on had the sitar lessons, to be a part of the Diwali celebrations. It was much appreciated by the parents and it was absolutely marvellous.

16

I started my schooling in January 1973 at the very westernised Sir Jonathon North Girls school, and fortunately my head teacher was very fond of Asian culture because she used to go up and down India, and she got all the Asian girls together... literally in the whole school there were eight girls, and she wanted us to do some dances and all the other girls had never done any dance so I was in charge. I started choreographing for these eight girls at school, probably I was 13 years old, and every term we used to present a dance at the school which I prepared. I used to find the recorded music from friends and the family, I used to prepare during lunchtime. So I started really, choreographing... from the age of 13.

I knew I was ready to enter the competitions, I mean it took a lot of convincing because my father was very autocratic, very orthodox. For him, dance and music... are not prospects for careers, so I had a lot of problems. But they did allow me to participate and when I went to the training - we had intensive training by dancers who had come from Uganda who used to prepare dances there... we all had to have some input to prepare the dances and the costumes. from there I went to learn Kathak dance, at a very old age I should say, with Nilima Devi, who started her institute sometime in 1981 or 1982. With lots of responsibilities and commitments I could not give 100% to this art style, I realised it was much more difficult than folk dancing. Folk dancing became a piece of cake for me.

From late 1980s... dance came into school, which was introduced I believe by Mrs Devi. She used to take me to some of the schools to assist her in folk dancing. It was very new to teach dance in the school to English little boys and girls but I think it's become very successful.

Members of the Shenton Dance Group   *Mrs D. Bahra*

**The Shenton Dance Group was formed in the early 1980s, and was
the first multicultural group to promote Asian Dance (Raas, Garba
and Bhangra). The group was comprised of teachers from Shenton
Primary School, and through their performances they raised
awareness of Asian dance to children within schools and to the
local communities, as well as breaking down racial barriers.
Members of the group also helped to raise funds for charity.**

**The co-ordinator of the group, Deedar Bahra, also organised a
childrens' dance group for pupils of Abbey and Shenton Primary
schools.**

Children of Abbey Primary School   *Mrs D. Bahra*

The 1980s

'To promote our music, our culture,
get it known to our people'

The 1980s saw the beginning of the structure of teaching that we see in Leicester today. From the major arts venues and the City and County Councils, to individual teachers in schools, colleges and at home, the teaching and promotion of dance and music slowly began to flourish. One important development at this time was the establishment of the UK's first Asian Dance Animation project in 1985 - an active partnership between Leicester City Council, Leicestershire County Council, East Midlands Arts and The Arts Council. The scheme was set up to promote awareness of Asian dance and to develop training and performance programmes. At the same time, the Asian Dance Support Group was founded to provide support to the Animation project, and as a platform for community involvement. Another local organisation, Shruti Arts, was also set up to bring Indian dance and music to Leicester.

A performance by the folk musicians from Rajastan, organised by Shruti Arts
Leicester Mercury

Since my childhood I was very much involved in musical activities and I came to know that Leicester will be the ideal place for me... before settling down here in 1977 I'd visited the country several times, you know, so I knew from my previous visits... I found that it is something like Africa, there is no hustle and bustle, you know, like London, if you want to visit a place... it takes one hour, two hours. You take appointments here, you drive down to Oadby and if the person isn't there, it's okay, forget it! Just 10 or 15 minutes.

Pop music was quite popular then. Activities in folk music were going on, not very much, but, you know. Not many groups were functioning. As far as classical music was going... activities were negligible I would say. Before I came I heard from my friends... that they had invited some artists who were visiting from India to arrange private sessions. I'm a singer, I play harmonium and sing... light music, and that involved me with a lot of people - good contacts it established. My main area is classical music, I'm very fond of classical music, so I thought that if we were to develop this field here in Leicester then we should get together. Not one or two individuals can do anything much, you know... so we got together. You'll laugh but at that time what used to happen, individuals used to invite classical artists or any main artists to their homes and even when the artist was performing they used to collect money for him. I mean, no artist would perform free... a small remuneration would be appreciated. It was becoming too much, it was not the right manner, you know, this is what encouraged us to form one club. We formed Shruti Arts which is here to promote Indian classical music, South Asian dance and music. It worked very well.

We were not worried about venues. In order to do small concerts we thought there are plenty of venues. But now, since we grew, we find venues a real problem in Leicester now, especially for dramas. At that time, for smaller concerts, 100, 150, 200 people, there were a lot of school halls... we have used very much the Moat Community College hall. One big event for us especially was the all night concert, arranged by us, Shruti Arts, at Soar Valley College. That was really a wonderful experience for us.

I would say there are, from the sub-continent of India especially, three musical styles that are very popular - in the west I would say it's the same thing. One is folk music, which comes from your roots, second thing is pop music which is from the cinema - all this rock music etc, you know - third is... this Indian classical music, which is not very popular, but certainly it's the root of all music, which is a serious music.

Bamboo flute... sitar, santoor which has got 100 strings, all these instruments are quite special instruments. When I came those instruments were not available. People used to go to India and bring those instruments with them when they travelled. There were one or two shops, you know, selling one or two harmoniums but not a big variety or anything, no. Nowadays there are a few shops in Leicester, Birmingham or London, you know, people don't get stuck.

We started Shruti Arts in '83 and we had the first inaugural concert, in fact on our premises here. Small gathering... and we had something like a turnout of 60, 70 people, but it was very well received by those 70 people who came and that actually then started it off to make it into a proper group, to start off with an executive committee and have a membership group etc. At that time we started off with ten members, out of which all ten were actually involved with bringing it on. This was... not on a commercial basis but actually to promote our music, our culture, get it known to our people. It was amazing to see how many people were interested when you actually made it more public.

At that time we did about three or four concerts a year maximum... we just worked on membership money and at the end of the year you didn't have any money left and you started all over again, you know, those were good days. The major aim at that time was just music and dance, and mainly music. It was more like you invited your friends, and their friends, and it was in your lounge where you could only put in about 40 people, and then if you didn't have enough money to pay the artist you paid it out of your own pocket etc. But this way they could be more adventurous, call more famous artists etc. who will ask for more fees, and it took off the ground.

I'm sure all of us, inside us, have that feeling that we want to show something of ourselves outside, to the host community or to any other community, because now we are part of Britain, the Asian community is very much part of Britain, I mean, my own children... they are born and brought up here. I really think that we needed a niche for ourselves but that wasn't the main aim, I think a lot of it was, we were - personally this is my feeling - is that you feel insecure because you don't feel you have anything of yourself, and you're still not fitting into the host community straight away either, so you need something for yourself to keep you going.

The first concert that we had was Hariprasad Chaurasia and Zakir Hussain. Now they are very big names and even at that time the fee was £500, 14 years ago £500 was a lot of money, and we used to think how are we going to manage this? Are we going to have people coming in? It was good - four or five of them, Chandu Bhai, Dr Hirani, Mr Varu, there were four or five people like that got together and said, well don't worry about it, if you make a loss we'll chip in, £50 each or whatever but we must do something... for our pleasure if nobody else's. It seemed like a lot of hard work because we didn't have a particularly posh venue.. we had to set up the stage, we had to do the hall up, it was all floor seating, it was here on our premises, yes. In that first year we had three or four concerts. Two or three years later we were doing six or eight concerts... names that weren't that well known either, but still people were coming in because they knew Shruti Arts was promoting something that was good. We could be more adventurous and actually call artists from India when we had an all night concert, when we went through from sort of nine in the evening till four in the morning and we had four different artists. I mean, that was quite a moment really.

It wasn't so expensive that only the elite could come, we kept it at an absolute minimum price so that if we could just cut even or make a £50 loss that was fine, we'd put in the £50 ourselves. It had to be at a level where everybody would think well I might as well try, it's only a couple of pounds... go and see it, and that's what we wanted people to do, just give it a go... we were quite confident that if they came once they were going to come back again. And 14 years on we've still got those members.

I was working until seven in the evening and then we came home and everybody got together at home and I'd cook dinner for them and, you know, we'd be posting out and writing - I mean we didn't have a computer - we'd write all the addresses out. It was fun, we all worked together to achieve something.

At that time Phoenix Arts was revamping their whole centre and I remember I'd applied for a job there as the liaison officer in terms of dance etc. That was in fact in 1980. That's when I knew a little bit that they wanted to promote it more. Apart from that, not very much else happening.

In the beginning, what they wanted, an Asian person basically, to get into the Asian part of developing in the community. The job... was to actually go out into the community and find... activities happening, maybe they were happening on their own, and what they wanted was to bring it all together at the Phoenix and maybe hold it as a centre. The person who'd taken on the job... Mohammed Raza he was very much involved... it did take time. A little bit reluctant I think (the community). Anything is new, I think all of us are quite reluctant to get involved but Mr Raza himself was, and is, very good at co-ordinating people and a lot of people knew him, so I think because he was there that helped to put that first step in. Initially... you always think.. do I really want to lose my independence? I think that's one thing that a lot... of the small community groups are worried about.

The Asian person.... the criteria was that you needed to speak two or three of the Asian languages, plus English, to communicate community wide really, and make it easily accessible. I mean, they had leaflets out but they all were in English and so maybe they didn't get to the right people, and this was what they were trying to do. I mean, I don't think they had any realisation as how much there was outside. The whole point really, I think the first year, was spent finding what was available outside and what then they can do with it.

I was teaching dance at a school... teaching the teachers and then the teachers could bring it into the school itself, which was very nice to see that a little bit of the culture was going in. And once that started, a couple of years later started the home school liaison officers which I was involved in, which brought in culture - if not dance and music - I mean, it brought in festivals and people got to know about Diwali, Eid, etc. which was then being slowly introduced into the schools as a celebration, including Christmas. All this... say, from '82-'87.

In fact the two schools... that I was involved with in the Highfields area, they accepted me very quickly because they were crying out for such things but there wasn't anybody available to them; they didn't know who to approach or what to do basically. I remember we were about three or four home liaison officers in different schools and it was nice, I mean, I was just fresh out of university, you know, all with ideas and the determination to do something. There was a lot of support from the teachers and the heads in those particular schools, which were sort of 90% Asian basically - Green Lane Infants and Bridge Junior.

Opportunities to learn dance and music also became available at community and social centres like the Shree Sanatan Centre.

Firstly we started that in 1982, and then I was the first chairman. We began with limited funds and gradually we got some grant from the Sports Council, when we bought some equipment... then we saw the demand was there because in that area there was a lot of Asians living, and there was no facilities... so we gradually started organising properly, and developing, and we asked for more grant from the City Council, so they provided us with the staff and running expenses. Now we have got everything there in the community centre. We are teaching them properly, you know... harmonium classes, tabla

Dance class at the Shree Sanatan Centre
Ian Whittaker

classes, vocal classes, dances, Raas Garba, flower making... Gujarati also. So gradually we built up, we've got over 1,000 members there. It took a number of years, you know, to develop that... nearly 15 years.

The 1980s saw teachers coming from outside Leicester. One of the people most instrumental in teaching classical dance in Leicester since 1980 has been Nilima Devi.

I started inquiring. I came to know that at Belgrave one lady teaches dance... I heard that she's not teaching on a regular basis. I started doing a lot of inquiries to find if I could have any connection with Indian dance. I couldn't find anybody so I thought, okay, let me start my own school now... that was my idea in India after my masters degree. What happened... we had a beautiful shed at the back because the house we were living in, it was a Polish butcher's shop... and the back of the shed they used to smoke the sausages. I told my husband, look, why don't we make this into a studio. On 1 January 1981 I started teaching there.

A lot, a lot of young ladies came... not young children but young ladies, who were 22, 23... who were always looking for someone to teach (them). I started with three students on the very first day and then hundreds came later on. What happened was, the news spread all over the place, so in the community, in schools, everybody started calling me to give demonstrations, give workshops, this and that. Sometimes I had to do free of charge just to develop interest, let people know, you know.

They were not young mothers, they were young girls who were sort of, after their studies they were doing a full time job somewhere else and they wanted to do evening work, you know, some kind of hobby. Within two years of their training I started putting them on the stage. In India we would never do it like that unless they were very well trained but here, just to create interest in the community I started putting them on the stage. Like that it spread and spread. That was up to '84.

In 1985 East Midland Arts contacted City Council, County Council, and Arts Council of Britain, and gathered funding to establish an animateur post in Leicester. In fact, the dance officer of East Midlands Arts knew me very well... and she said that, 'I am looking for two sorts of things, one is for the folk and one is for the classical. We are looking at two part-time posts.' So in 1985... I took up a classical dance animateur post.

In the beginning... people didn't know anything. They thought that Kathak is a film dance... they couldn't even differentiate what is folk and what is classical. They know what is Raas and Garba but they wouldn't know it was a folk dance. I feel that one thing is that people here who are from Africa, I think they have lost touch with India and they are not aware of this rich cultural heritage of India and they cannot see how dance is part and parcel of the culture. That is why, when I started working as an animateur I established this Introduction to Indian Dance leaflet.

What happened, it was a big boost to work. Because of this post we had to give free services, so there was a huge waiting list of going for workshops and lectures, demonstrations. I did a lot of work in schools, many schools, and what happened,

Bharatnatyam
dancer
Chitra Bolar

the demand became so huge, intense, people used to call us from neighbourhood centres - can you run a workshop or can you start a class... we opened a lot of classes in different places in Leicester.

Some parents were reluctant... because some girls wanted to learn and their parents were not happy, so sometimes we went to parents' houses to convince them. But some fathers were very strong and very much of traditional beliefs, you know, that no we do not consider dance a respectable thing and we do not want our daughter to learn. They do not see, because what happened, during medieval times in India, the northern part of India was especially affected when the dance moved from temple to the court, and the position of dance became, sort of, instead of a religious and cultural message, it became an entertainment. It degraded so much during that time that it was considered to be prostitution. And also, in Hindi films... during that time (1980s) video culture was very popular in Leicester, and they used to see all the time films on video. And in the video they see all these dances and they're not proper classical but they're a mixture of everything, and... when they portray dance as a very cheap entertainment parents think, oh this is the dance my daughter is going to learn. It is very difficult to educate such fathers and mothers.

When I came here it was a different experience for me, teaching from India to here. In India we teach twice a week or we teach every day. Here I started twice a week class. In the beginning some young girls came, later on they said, oh it is getting too much for us, we can't do twice a week, can't we keep it once a week? Another thing I noticed here, there was a quick drop out, even though they would come with enthusiasm to learn... if I started a class of ten by the end of two months or three months I would end up with two or three. Because if they wouldn't know the nature of the dance they wouldn't know the kind of training they were receiving and it was completely, maybe, out of

Leicester City Council

Kathak maestro and choreographer, Kumidini Lakhia, came to Leicester in 1993 and led masterclass workshops at the Shree Sanatan Centre

expectation, what they were doing. So some of them used to drop out, you know, because it needs a lot of mental and physical discipline, concentration, it needs a lot of energy, it needs patience, and one needs really to enjoy that sort of thing. Most of them, I think, found it very difficult, and some of them came with the expectation that in two weeks time they would learn it.

When I saw this drop out, in the beginning it used to hurt me. Some young people, they used to learn six months and then they would go, and some for one year, one and a half... you use to feel, 'Why didn't they tell me?' That is another attitude, like in India at least they would say, 'Sorry we can't,' but here the attitude was very different. So I thought, okay, I must give them an aim... but they were coming once a week, so I looked at my Indian syllabus and it was very hard because I could see it was every day coming and training. So I thought, let me set up a course according to once a week, so I set up a training course for them and I made a six year diploma. That helped, that encouraged many young students to continue up to three years, four years.

As time passed I thought, I can't teach every evening and every day. The dance officer of East Midlands Arts told me that I should, with some of my advanced students, start a trainee animateur course. Then they can be trained to teach the grass root level work in the community. I started that training I think in '87. Within three years they had a lot of opportunity to work with professional artists in different classical styles, and a lot of teachers and dancers who were visiting from India, they learnt a lot of different folk dance, and I think it developed with a lot of enthusiasm and confidence.

In '81-'85 I did a lot a lot of outreach work within schools and the community but I also did a lot of consistent work at my school; '85-'90 I was more out... a lot of outreach work. Within that we created a lot of performance work, we trained a lot of groups... did a lot of work with visiting artists, lectures, demonstrations, plus festivals. We were involved in Abbey Park festival, then schools festivals, you know, Diwali festivals, then sometimes Holi festivals but that was not very prominent. Maybe in schools our role became important... as part of Holi festival they wanted us to go and give a talk and sort of do a dance or create movements for the Holi story, Prahlad and Holika, and I used to choreograph the movements for the children.

Other teachers arrived and had similar experiences to Nilima Devi. Although there was great enthusiasm there was also an ignorance of classical dance and the feeling that dance was to be no more than a hobby or pastime.

I was invited by the Education Authority of Leicester to come and take charge of the project known as the Indian Music Project that was funded by the County Council and based at the old School of Music building at the Rowans. I came as advisor of music. My responsibility was to make sure the dance project was running well... and at the same time looking after the music side as well.

People at that time were very curious, you know, wherever I used to go, 60, 70, 100 students would come and... to talk to me. At that time I think there was a bit of a buzz, as well - oh, there's a classical dancer has come from India and he's young and we all want to learn. But they didn't have a clue. I used to ask them, 'Do you know any classical dances?' and they used to go, 'Yes yes, we all know classical dances.' 'What is that?' 'Well there are two classical dances here.' 'Yes?' 'One is Garba, one is Bhangra.' So that was their understanding at the time. People who are living in the west who came from Africa, they were involved in music but what sort of music they were doing they didn't know. They wouldn't know a huge difference between... film music, or cheap music and good classical music. It's a matter of building a taste. There are so many kinds of music and I'm sure people enjoy music... it has to be appreciated on all levels, but people should also understand... which is a high level of music. It will only get better if people learn. Enthusiasm-wise I never had a problem, it was the opposite. There was never a shortage of people, in fact I had to tell them no I can't take you.

I think my first school was Abbey Primary... and then East Park. I used to visit all the 6th form colleges and secondary schools with other music teachers, to assist them. At the same time we used to do... like a demonstration performance every Friday morning, I must have done over 200, all over the... county. So they used to see my performance and get very hyped up, interested, and when I used to go there they were all there.

Dance was introduced after a year. I produced dances... from then on things really went from strength to strength. Every event at that time was very very important. We used to do mostly showcases. I mean, when I see the videos now... I think, my God! maybe I was banging my head against the wall at that time to teach people at that level, but it still was worth it, what we did. Very basic.

Display of Dandiyas (sticks) during Navratri

Teaching mudras (hand gestures)

It was good... there was a cultural life, but obviously compared to India it wasn't much so I was a bit shocked at first, I thought, is this it, just that many people, and small activities going on. Slowly, I realised... at least there's something going on, it's better than nothing. Dance-wise and music-wise it wasn't like India, you know, activities going on every week, it wasn't like that, it was particularly for Navratri festival and Diwali and things like that.

Within a week I went to the Spinney Hill Centre... they found out I am a classical dancer and I'm willing to teach here. They had some show at Spinney Hill and they asked me to perform there... and I did my first performance there and they said... we really want this sort of activity in this area, if you don't mind and if you can teach us. That's how I started my first class in Spinney Hill. Particularly, that area, I didn't see any classes that were there, no music class, no dance classes, and the people, especially children, were really willing to learn something. There used to be some sort of dance event in the school, but in the community... they wanted something in the community centre. At the same time I met Nilima... and she introduced me to the Bhagini Centre, which is a women's centre.

Bharatnatyam - I don't think there was anyone else, because the first problem, what I found when I did my performance... people started asking me, oh we would like to learn this Kathak dance, and I says, 'This is not Kathak, this is Bharatnatyam.' Then I thought, no, there is this sort of difficulty that... they don't know the difference between Kathak and Bharatnatyam because probably they didn't see much Bharatnatyam here because Kathak was at that time well established... especially in Leicester. So I had to explain to them, and they said, 'Oh it's classical dance, it's all the same.' And I say it's basically the same but if you think about it there is a lot of difference. I had to explain all the time.

First... it was all beginners, and especially, like, some of the children, or some of the parents, didn't know the difference, they just wanted their children to learn something, you know, like some sort of hobby, or because, some children I found, they were being naughty in the house and parents wanted them to leave for a couple of hours... some sort of baby-sitting thing, and that was really annoying. Some children, especially younger children, they didn't want to come, their parents used to force them. I had to explain to them, look, it's not going to work like this.

Dance training... obviously it's very similar to ballet. They have to do the basic warming up exercise, and basic footwork and hand movements - all the physical exercise they have to do before they actually learn the dance. And then, eventually they have to establish their footwork, and hand movement, hand gestures, facial expressions, and everything. So it is a very long training, you know, it's not that they can learn it in ten or 20 weeks and in this country people expect that they just learn it in ten weeks and the child should be on the stage and that's where we have to face the difficulties.

You shouldn't actually compare, but again, if you try to compare, it is different, because in India... the tradition is there, the culture is there, so there you don't have to teach culture to the children, they already know... so you just have to train them about the dance. But in this country, first of all the language problem; because although... the children, they can speak English very fluently, no problem, when they have to speak their own mother tongue they... sort of, you know, won't talk properly or they won't come out properly. So obviously in *any Indian classical dance the language is the most important because we use a Sanskrit language and that is, it's not hard... but for this country's children it is hard. I have to explain the meaning... how you pronounce the words and the sentences, so it is difficult. Other thing is the culture, they have a little knowledge... but still it's not as wide as India, so you have to tell them about the culture... the importance of the culture... guide them towards the right impression and the right way. I used to think, 'Oh wait a second, why can't they speak their own mother tongue', when I came here... but now I realise... I think it's the parents' fault - if they don't talk in their own mother tongue inside the home then it's not the children's fault. It's the parents' duty to sort of introduce about Asian culture and Asian languages.*

Sometimes we really have to struggle because some theory, okay they can do all the theory in English, but sometimes some of the pronunciation - it's very easy to explain them in an Asian language rather than in English because it's the meaning - it's a little bit changed when you try to explain them in English. And when you try to explain them in the Indian language it's very difficult because they don't understand most of the things. We have to do three or four roles at the same time - as a dance teacher, as a culture teacher, as a language teacher.

It took off for me when I eventually became Head of Rushey Mead Comprehensive, not right at the beginning in 1985, but I would say three or four years into the job I got more and more involved - I mean a lot of things to do with Asian culture you're living, breathing every day in terms of the youngsters in the school - and I made a positive effort... to get out into the community. Because I actually went out to a lot of events I eventually got involved in the Asian Dance Support Group in... probably '88, '89.

Dance itself... is somewhat marginalised in the sense of what actually happens in most schools. I'm not particularly talking South Asian dance, I'm talking any dance, and Rushey Mead was no exception to that. It was a school that had a very small amount of dance, mainly for girls in the junior part of school, and I decided that this was unsatisfactory so I pushed very hard to try and improve dance generally in the school. We're marginally better than we were, to be quite honest with you, we do have it built in now with our PE curriculum through years seven, eight and nine, for boys and girls.

But what I really felt was if we were going to move on this then what we really needed to do was tap into this rich vein of what was going on, basically, outside the school and around, so what I managed to do was work with people like Nilima Devi and some of her dance animateurs to come in on occasions and do some set work with small groups, not everybody. There was at that time... the capacity to actually demonstrate the art so everybody in the school was aware of what was going on and what the potential was, and it really gave our students then an opportunity to a little bit of their own - if they were keen they could join a club or get some extra help in school, if they were very very keen then they would be able to join into a community activity, either through the Belgrave Community Centre or whatever. So what it managed to do was build a general interest and involvement and give the students at least a sense whereby if you want to take this further forward these are the opportunities we can give you.

The 1990s

*'It has enriched Leicester's culture,
it has enriched Asian culture...'*

**The public's knowledge of Asian dance and music has
increased considerably. Now, in the 1990s, there is a depth of
appreciation and participation that is far greater than in the
1960s. However, although the enthusiasm is evident, some
people feel that high standards have still to be attained,
particularly in the music field.**

I would say interest was there... I am very pleased that at some of the
concerts we have at Phoenix Arts and other places we regularly get the
host community and they are enjoying this music. As I say, Pandit Ravi
Shankar, he is the one who created interest. Whites were aware of the

Indian musical instruments

Leicester Mercury

A young member of the
local youth music
association, Sangeet
Sabha, playing the tabla.

Indian music, you know, and they used to read reviews in the national papers of the concerts taking place at London... so they knew about this thing. I've seen so many whites regularly at our concerts.

I'm a specialist in Gujarati music, you know, which is a serious music, not folk, and not classical, but light music we call it. A couple of instruments. You can involve large groups for chorus singing and other things, you know... but I mainly concentrated on my own singing style where not many musicians are involved - three or perhaps four, you know, that will be sufficient. Harmonium, tabla player, a guitar player and one or two side rhythm, that will be fine. If I can get more instruments that would be very nice, you know, like flute... but it's very difficult. This place, especially Leicester, we haven't got good musicians you know. I'm talking about Indian music... you will find for this popular film music, you will find keyboard players or a few guitar players, but you wouldn't find any sitar players who can accompany you... there are only one or two people who are deeply involved in classical music, not for accompaniment, you know, so you wouldn't find a flute player, you wouldn't find a violin player. If I want to produce an album here it will be a problem for me, I won't find good musicians here... I mean 'good' means a really good standard, you know. I go to India, yes, even now. London yes, but not as good as India. I'll give you a simple example... last month I was in India to produce a new CD and I was just wondering, what a quality we have in India, you know, and the reason is simple - there is tough competition, you have to be the best to survive. Unfortunately in this country people who play music - I'll be very blunt - they are not doing their right training, or riyaz, as we call it, their practice, you know, and they get their contracts very quickly and they jump into their concerts straight away. So the standard is still not that good here.

Classical is a fixed pattern, they follow the old words and some of their ragas and we call this bandish which is taught by the guru, you know, that has been going on since centuries. As far as film music is concerned... they have these modern film lyric writers, they write these words... which are very common, you know. My particular one... these modern poets in India, they write good poetry which has got some good meanings which you can thoroughly enjoy. We follow this pattern. Subjects are very many, not just one or two... love songs, family songs, religious songs.

I am glad about one thing in Leicester... that is the Indian music being taught in the schools. That has created new, young musicians. The only thing I'm not happy about is that something more should be done, I mean, primary level they are doing fine but for their further education in music there is no scope in Leicester. On a higher level something should be done.

Classical dance teachers, like Nilima Devi, have continued to develop their work.

By 1990 I realised a lot of work was happening but there was no consistent work. Even my own work at the Institute was slowing down, I couldn't get much time to teach there.

I realised that not everyone who comes to learn classical is full of potential. I thought, okay, it's much better if they learn outside and if they are really keen they can come to me. What happened, I looked at the Knighton Fields role model of ballet where they used to take children... from the age of seven, eight... so I thought why not, I'll develop this side. By 1990 I started establishing this project at the Knighton Fields centre but not at my school. Within five years we have got nearly 70 children coming through this system. At the Knighton Fields centre I encourage young children who are doing well to take exams. The role of my school has changed, it has become a place of advanced training and for an examination level of training.

What is happening, when I started the training animateur class in Leicester, it was not only my students in Leicester who were involved, there were students... from Nottingham they used to come here. Now some of them are teaching in Nottingham and Derby and what is happening - very interesting - they are so strong in believing that our students learn from us, that they must come to me for advanced training. So they are keeping that sort of relationship.

My brief to look at the community dance is to sort of create an interest in dance as a hobby, and they learn a kind of skill that they can perform on stage. So I thought, okay, fine, not everybody is going to go to a certain level. They are learning.. they are enjoying... they are performing here and there, fine... don't force them. Maybe at the end of the day if they are serious they want to do it, otherwise not.

It has developed a lot because when I came here... there wasn't much Bharatnatyam activity going on... it was all about Kathak and, obviously, there was folk dance and community dance. First couple of years up to '90 I started working in so many community centres... then I started doing lots of shows in schools and community centres... and demonstrations as well. And after that, in the last four or five years, there are about four or five Bharatnatyam dancers came from India and all of a sudden the Bharatnatyam is there, and now people have got awareness about Bharatnatyam and the difference between the different styles of dance. There is awareness and it's developed a lot.

In my private class now... I thought why don't we set an examination here. There is one exam board in London... I spoke to them... and now my students are taking exams. They have the aim, they have the goal, and they have a direction. They are learning and hopefully they will achieve some diploma.

Unfortunately we can't get live music here, that's a really annoying thing because in India we have live musicians - even during the training we have live musicians there so that's really good - but here even in performance we have to use tapes. It doesn't feel right, you can't come out properly. North Indian musicians, you can find lots of musicians here, but South Indian, I mean, in Leicester I don't think there is any... in London and Birmingham you do, but not in Leicester. Flute, they use violin, and it's very similar to tabla, but it's called mridangam. Again, the music has its difference as well, the north Indian and south Indian music.

I had one experience... one of my students she was really clever... and there was one performance... and just before the performance I said, 'By the way, you know you'll have to wear Ghungru, the ankle bells.' And she came the following day and she said, 'Sorry, I can't do the performance.' I said, 'Why not?' She goes, 'I can't wear the Ghungru... my father wouldn't like me to wear that... because my father thinks the prostitute who just dances in front of men and tries to please them, they wear these Ghungru... that's a bad symbol.' That

*really hurt me... before we put it on we always pray, after we finished our show
we take it off and we pray again, so we pay respect. I did try to tell him...
explain to him. He did understand but still inside he had a doubt. He wouldn't
mind if someone else wears it but not his own daughter, it was like that.*

I think it's lifestyle, that's what I think. Because here, husband and wife,
both are working, and they've got to work otherwise you can't live here. I
mean, you haven't got much time to do these sorts of things. In India... it's
totally different there. Dance and music come from culture... if there is a culture
then the music and dance comes.

It is developing quite nicely. The efforts they are making... they are creating
new things. If I talk in particular of my students, they are developing, but in
general they've got lots of diversions to go on. There's computer games, sports,
gym, lots of things there so you can't just tell them music and dance.

I'll tell you one example: my students, they went to one show and they saw
this film dance - Raja film dance - and their... parents, they don't know if this is
classical dance or is film dance. 'Do you like this Indian dance?' her mum asked
her and she said, 'That's not Indian dance, they haven't got the Mudras and
everything.' So that's the point, they know what is Indian dance and what's
film dance, and about Mudras and Taal, so they are developing.

*It's a bit difficult because many people wouldn't really think of dance as a
career, especially here, it's a very difficult line to choose.*

It's not considered manly, I mean if you see some of the male dancers
nowadays you wouldn't think they are men really, so it doesn't look like a good
attraction for us boys. What you need is a sort of... boy Kathak dancers who
show some sort of... more powerful, which is more attractive to boys. It's very
difficult because if I tell some of my friends I do dance they're like, 'Huh?' You
know, 'What is this?' And especially if it's classical - if you do Bhangra it's okay,
I mean anyone can do that - it's just classical dance is really a dying art form
among the boys. We have to find a new way of making it attractive. A very
difficult job. It requires a lot of commitment, I don't think many boys are ready
to give that.

**As well as the work in community centres and schools there are
now several private Indian dance and music schools in Leicester,
such as Kumar Saswat's Sampa Centre.**

This place, which is known as Sampa - set up in 1993 - the prime target is
to create a performer. We are not only interested in teaching but we want to
see someone come up as a full scale performer. It is all self-financed and it
teaches the highest degree of music and dance. Subjects we are offering here:
tabla, pakhawaj, Kathak dance, sitar, santoor, flute, shehnai, vocal, and it is
already become quite a high profile place.

The reputation of Leicester is very good and that's why things are
happening. What is happening in Leicester is because of all the years of work
that have been done by so many people, and it is the time and place to be
artistically, I mean, there's a lot to be done, still a lot to be done...

Performance of Bedla folk dance

Performance of Tippani folk dance

Well I think it's progressed in that... there is a greater awareness of this, in the sense of crossing boundaries. I think that particularly through the Asian dance support group we have managed, to an extent, to do some sharing so there will be one group who might have been only associated with Kathak will now at least maybe get along to a production, you know, a folk presentation or whatever. So I think generally... there is more sharing, more awareness of what's going on, and I think it does push it. I think it's one of these things that's really very marginalised and unless you've got a driving force behind it, like a support group to keep pushing it forward, I think it will slip back. You've only got to think of the example of how hard someone like Nilima Devi has to work... to keep all those things on the go, there's not a lot of money in it, you know. That sort of - I've given Nilima as an example - development needs a lot of support. So I think we've managed to keep it on the agenda and keep it moving forward, and when we have these big showcases, again it's a really good example for people to come along.

I'll give an example of what I think is very positive here (Rushey Mead School). We have, every year, a kaleidoscope of different dance, drama, music activities and we actually just invite the youngsters within their own particular interest groups to come forward and present what they want to present... and we always are inundated with requests to do South Asian dance.

Of course some of the productions and presentations go on through the Haymarket or the Phoenix or whatever. There was some speculation... there was so much interest in the showcase example that we do each year they were thinking of De Montfort Hall as a sort of venue because so many people want to come along. And certainly some of our youngsters, I mean I think we've got one of the trophies over there now, they actually go far and wide with their own groups out of Leicester. There are national competitions.

From a casual hobby to a way of life, dance and music mean different things to different people

I feel that Indian classical dance and music... why they are solo, because it is to lead towards realisation, it's another medium, it's another path, to lead towards the realisation, towards the light. Because they call it tapashcharya. Tapashcharya means a kind of training, it's like a meditation, it's a yoga, when you train yourself you are completely absorbed in your tapashcharya and you are bringing soul, mind and body together, then you become one... it is sort of bringing the self towards realisation. That is my philosophy... because when I look at it more and more I see dance like that, but now the role has changed because it has become a part of culture, teaching identity, teaching as a physical exercise. So I see a very broad role.

Dance and music is everything, it's my life and I'm very proud to be born in a family where music has been given me as an inheritance. There's nothing like music. Yes, the profession is very hard, you have to be absolutely good to survive, otherwise tough, very tough. Here, everybody's doing well, well in the sense that they are all busy performing, teaching at their level, whatever their level.

Performance of "Rainbow" by
students of the Institute of Classical
Indian Dance at Phoenix Arts in 1994

Leicestershire and in particular Leicester City Council have gone out of their way to try and fund some of the events and encourage the multicultural part of Leicestershire's community. Asian dance has played a great role on the... performing arts front over the last ten, 15 years. They have also brought in elements of how to... involve the wider community - not just Leicester but the whole of Leicestershire, so Leicester City Council itself ought to be thanked. It has enriched Leicester's culture, it has enriched Asian culture, it has enriched the whole of the west in some ways. It is put on the tourist guide of Leicester... if anything Asian is put on a tourist guide of Leicester City it can be only a credit to our culture.

I think it is very important. Nowadays most of the parents, and the children as well, are aware of what Asian dance means. The community are really interested and they have more awareness of it. I think it is really a bridge to get their culture back... it is through entertainment so people like to learn more that way.

Before, the western community thought that dance was only for Asians. Now, they've become more aware that anybody can do it, it's available for everybody... in the classical style as well as the folk style. Even if they don't want to learn they just want knowledge about it, and they're fascinated just by the knowledge. Another thing that has developed is that before we used to dance in very minor community centres for small audiences... sometimes very poor conditions, in the parks, in the gardens. But now the development is that Asian dance goes to the theatre, even the folk dances go to the theatre... yes, it went to De Montfort Hall but that had to be a competition, now it doesn't have to be a competition, people have their groups and they can go to theatres. And more and more parents are allowing their children to participate in dance. Before, that was a difficult problem as well. There were very small groups taking part, now everybody wants to learn dance.

Extremely important, because as far as I'm aware, all of the East African Asians have... really settled in Leicester. Because East Africa was very forward in the cultural activities it was they who brought this culture back, so if we look at Leicester it's more like East Africa, because the people are the same and they didn't want to forget about their culture, they didn't want to drop it.

Here we have only - life is in certain ways so limited... for some people it's very mechanical, life here, because, from work to home and home to work, if they are married they are both working so they haven't got any spare time, so therefore it is important that if they have a hobby, or a knowledge of this music and dance, then they can enjoy their life better in their spare time. So therefore I see that it is essential that everyone should have knowledge of this so that they can mix properly in the community, they can participate in the community, also they can understand the culture, and they can make their life better and more enjoyable.

This Asian music and dance is one of the arts which is very useful. Without that and the language you can't keep your identity, and you can't understand the root of your existence. In order to understand the culture and roots you need to know your musical background, and your cultural background, and your language background. Without that you are not a perfect human as far as I can see.

I've seen children sort of grow up in different parts of Leicester. In some parts they were exposed to the culture, in other parts they were not. You can see the difference between these children. By saying that I mean some children probably lived in areas where there was maybe 98, 99% indigenous children so there were no cultural activities as such, so these children would grow up totally lacking any knowledge of our culture, and not only that, sometimes later on they were refusing to be involved with the culture. Whereas the children who have grown up in schools... where they have been exposed to the culture, they developed pride in that and a lot of them have gone on to develop their own skills further and be more actively involved. I think the ones who were not involved have lost out in some ways.

It's a sort of public face of Asian culture - that one organised in the '70s already, these sort of multicultural meetings. The significant thing was it wasn't people sitting round a table and discussing cultures, it was people showing to each other what their culture involved, and I know this happened in other areas, I mean people had food tasting sessions, people had dress changing sessions, if you like, and so you were trying on a sari or a dhoti or what have you. That happened a lot in the '70s, it's still going on now a bit. They actually went out and introduced it to everybody. Asians wanted to be seen to be a part of the whole thing.
I think it's less visible in Leicester, I mean it's there, but it's much more in Birmingham for example where you have Bhangra culture... because we are a Gujarati city in a sense, we are Gujarati dominated, and so the Asian culture here is different from Nottingham or Birmingham.

I think it is, main thing, important as a part of... their identity. It's a very good pastime/hobby for them, and it's very good developing a kind of skill which they can share with each other, which they can enjoy with each other. But if you look at it in general now, I think so many children are getting trained, and they perform within their own community, the standard has gone up. We are educating the wider area now. We have done at lot of work but I think, still, a lot of work needs to be done because what now we are looking at, we are looking at the national picture for South Asian dance development. I think Leicester is in many ways doing a lead role. I think we have established a very structured development... very slow but very gradual structured steps, and if you want to look at the dance as a full time training within three, four, years time it is possible.

Into the future

*'I want to make people so good that people
will be invited from here to India'*

I mean, what, at the end of the day, is British? If people start performing
Bharatnatyam to Beethoven music, or whatever... is that British? It is to
some extent, it's a hybrid development of cultures and you see that
everywhere I think. If you think of how people put together folk dance
performances or something like that, I think the emphasis is on recreating
tradition in some sense, and remembering tradition. From the beginning I
think a lot of people have been concerned about losing these things, and
so their efforts have been attempts to try and recreate and teach the
youngsters how these things work. Some people have become defensive
and said no we don't want to taint this with all sorts of influences, and
other people have said we are in Britain all right, so we introduce this that
and the other. You'll never find agreement. This whole issue of
contemporary dance - does it have to have western elements in it to be
contemporary dance or is there such a thing as Indian contemporary
dance? Of course there is, but people have political arguments about that.

*It (musical crossover) should happen because... youngsters are living in
the west and they have the taste, there's nothing wrong about it. At the
same time they want to learn their background. I have done personally a
lot of work with western musicians and I enjoy it very much... it opens your
mind.*

People are really being encouraged by their families and their parents
to get into it, and they're enjoying it, so that certainly helps.

*I think culture's getting more important for everyone now, especially
with parents encouraging kids to go to temples, Gujarati classes, dance
lessons, music lessons, just within all that activity I think culture's getting
more important.*

The seeds are growing here... the past 15 years. It's still developing, it's
still growing, still expanding, so you wouldn't see as top quality artists here
as you would see in India, or tuition, or facilities, or teachers as well... so
you can tell there's bound to be a better standard of dance or music out
there than here. In future years we may produce excellent artists.

*I haven't come across a single student who come with his or her -
there are hardly any boys learning - with their own soul and say I'm really
interested in dance, I want to do something in dance, I want to train myself
in dance, I want to make a career in dance. Not a single student. I have
pushed everyone. Up to now, two students, pupils, I sent them to India... I
want to push my students.*
When I trained, I must say one thing... when I was doing the diploma

we started with 15 and at the end of the diploma we were only four, at the end of the six years. And when I was doing the degree we were three and I think I was the only one who was doing, in my year... I was the only one person continuing. So, I think to go into the profession, very few people take it in India as well.

I think this is the only place in England where this system is running, like going round schools and auditioning children. That is a plus point for Leicester. Another plus point is that we have got a concentrated Asian population in Leicester... the only thing is that we are not good at publicising our work or giving a higher profile, and that we need to look at.

I started at ten years, I started out just at a community centre, and then I progressed. I was encouraged by my parents to go further and then I went to do my exam levels. Then, because I started enjoying it more and I was learning a lot more as well, I carried on until now, I'm still doing Kathak dance. Why? Because... from just when I was three years old I was always dancing round the house and that so my parents encouraged me to go to one of the classes on Saturdays and from then on it just carried on. I do want to continue it but it's hard doing, you know, A-levels, and hopefully going to Uni, so I definitely want to continue practising... and maybe afterwards do a teacher's course or something. I won't stop!

I would say that it's not just continuing to do dance but also to develop it among the community more because it still needs a lot of development. So as soon as I get older I would carry on practising dance, become really proficient at it, then I would probably go out, like many other students have done... go and teach in different communities and then spread it a bit more.

It's very nice to know that the host community has taken it on very well, and there's a lot of integration between the two and you get a lot of east-west mixes now. You see a lot of them playing our music instruments and vice-versa. Our children are playing the oboes and the pianos etc. and getting somewhere with it and that combination is bringing on very well. That brings them along culturally as well, because the children then talk about all these events, and music has no barriers, no language barriers or anything, so each child is interested in each other's events that are happening, and that's the main aim really isn't it, to have that cultural mix in the community.

It's changed by leaps and bounds really. There is a lot of interchange between the two communities and that brings a lot of happiness all round because they understand each other's communities, I mean, understanding is what we need really. It's all visual and it's easier to communicate in those languages, in dance and music.

Our concept is totally different. Music is never completed unless there are three elements involved in it: dance, percussion and melody. There is a Sanskrit shloka... The definition of music is the dance, percussion and melody. Just playing a sitar or violin is not music. So here (Sampa) for example, if someone is learning dance then they understand, they learn vocal, they understand

International Kathak Dancer
Pandit Durgalal who performed
in Leicester 1989

Performance of "The Ugly Duckling" in Kathak style at the Haymarket Theatre in 1988
Nilima Devi

everything - everything is under one roof. What happens is, to become a good dancer you have to be a very good musician first; to become a good musician you have to be a good dancer - not necessarily physically dancing but understanding has to be there. Then your music will be rich, otherwise you are just averagely trying to copy and play.

There is still a lot needs doing here, a lot... I want to make people so good that people will be invited from here to India. It's already happening and it will happen more, definitely. There are a lot of people who are teaching who grew up in Leicester I think. I want to see the people in Leicester achieve such a high degree of music and art that people don't have to bring from outside.

INDIAN DANCE STYLES

For the people of the Indian sub-continent, dance has long been an important part of their cultural and religious life, reflecting a rich variety of traditions dating back more than 3000 years. From ancient times, dance and music were part of drama and used to teach people religious and mythological stories. Eventually dance became separated from drama as an art form and regional styles developed.

There are now seven styles of classical dance, which are based on ancient Sanskrit texts, each using different regional techniques, music, costumes and language. In addition, there are hundreds of folk and tribal dances, which are traditionally performed on occasions such as births, marriages, harvest, religious festivals, etc. Indian film dances have more recently become popularised; they usually incorporate a mixture of classical, folk and creative elements.

Keith Thomson Photography

Invocation
performed by
Kathak Youth
Dance Group

CLASSICAL DANCE

Indian classical dances are based on rigid rules and a complicated system of hand gestures and rhythmic patterns of foot movements. Technique plays an important part and dancers have to follow several years of formal training. The various dances depict stories of the Hindu gods, particularly Brahma, Vishnu and Shiva. With the exception of Kathakali, they are solo dances, the artist playing the parts of several characters in the story. However, a recent development is for group presentations, using modern stories and themes rather than ancient myths. The seven classical styles are:

Kathak from North India, uses mime and body techniques to tell stories. Much of Kathak dance is based on intricate rhythmic patterns and musical mathematics.

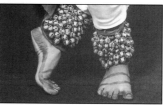

Ghungru Nilima Devi

Bharatnatyam named after Bharata's Natya Shastra, an ancient handbook of performing arts, this is a stylised dance using gesture (Mudra) language, from South India.

Odissi dancer Sanjukta Panigrahi

Kathakali a very dramatic dance from Kerala in South India, traditionally performed by a group of male dancers wearing elaborate head-dresses and painted make-up.

Mohiniattam from Kerala in South India, this is a female solo dance using techniques of both Bharatnatyam and Kathakali.

Manipuri a graceful dance from Manipur in the North East of India.

Odissi/Orissi this dance uses very stylised forms, influenced by the famous sculptures of temples in Orissa State, South East India.

Kuchipudi originating from Kuchipudi village in Andhra Pradesh, this is a classical dance/drama, usually performed as a female solo dance.

FOLK AND TRIBAL DANCES

A wide variety of folk dances have developed in villages all over India, usually to celebrate seasonal events. The most prominent folk dances performed in Leicester are those originating from Gujarat and Punjab:

Dandiya Raas   a Gujarati stick dance, performed by men and women, using circular movements and often danced to songs in praise of Lord Krishna.

Garba   a Gujarati clap dance, also using circular movements, and traditionally performed by women during the Hindu festival of Navratri in honour of the Goddess Amba.

Bhangra   a harvest dance from Punjab, usually performed by men, and incorporating vigorous and athletic movements. Bhangra has now become a popular disco style dance.

Giddha   an agricultural folk dance from Punjab, a very graceful dance performed by women using sophisticated hand and foot movements. It is rarely performed in public, but is enjoyed at weddings and social gatherings.

Other well known folk dances are: Manjira, Tippani, Lezim and Koli from West India; Raslila, Kumaon, Ghummar, Holi, Rouf and Nautanki from North India; Kolattam, Pinnal Kolottam, Vasanta Attam and Kummi from South India; Jatras, Kirtan, Baul dances, Mask dance of Bengal, Danda Nata and Stick dance from East India.

Originating from tribes in remote or mountainous areas of India, tribal dances are also performed to celebrate social and seasonal events. The Naga dances of Assam and the Gypsy dance of Rajasthan are among the most popular.

GLOSSARY

Bhajans	religious songs
Bandish	song text
Diwali	Hindu new year 'Festival of Lights'
Dhoti	traditional male trousers sometimes worn for dance performance or by Brahmins
Gangamaiya	a popular film song about a holy river in North India
Ghazal	light classical vocal music with Urdu text
Ghungru	dancing bells worn round the ankles
Holi	Hindu spring festival
Holika	Demon goddess
Kirtan	sung prayer
Mandir	Hindu temple
Manjira	small cymbals
Mridangam	percussion instrument
Mudra	hand gesture
Naal	percussion instrument
Navratri	Hindu festival performed over nine nights, with Garba and Raas dancing in honour of the goddess Amba
Pakhawaj	double-headed, barrel shaped wooden drum
Prahlad	son of the demon king Hiranya Kashipa
Riyaz	practice
Shehnai	double-reed wind instrument used in folk and classical music
Shloka	Sanskrit verse
Sitar	plucked lute-type stringed instrument
Santoor	musical instrument with 108 strings, played with two wooden sticks
Tabla	pair of drums; main percussion instrument in Indian classical music
Taal	rhythm